GRATITUDE
—— FOR KIDS ——

_____

Copyright © 2018 by M.H.Angelica

6th Birthday.

18 / 1 / 2020

MON	TUE	WED	THU	FRI	SAT	SUN
○	○	○	○	○	⊘	○

TODAY I AM GRATEFUL FOR...

1. My friends for coming.
2. For my presents.
3. My family and Sylvilians.

TODAY'S PEAKS:

I had fun on my birthday.

HOW HAPPY I FEEL: (second face circled – heart eyes)

SOMETHING AWESOME THAT HAPPENED TODAY:
DRAW OR WRITE ABOUT IT!

18 / 1 / 2020

MON TUE WED THU FRI **SAT** SUN

TODAY I AM GRATEFUL FOR...

1. for having sister.
2. for getting to bring Padraig.
3. having fun.

TODAY'S PEAKS:

having cake.

HOW HAPPY I FEEL: (second face circled — heart eyes)

SOMETHING AWESOME THAT HAPPENED TODAY:
DRAW OR WRITE ABOUT IT!

20 / 1 / 2020

MON ✓ TUE ○ WED ○ THU ○ FRI ○ SAT ○ SUN ○

TODAY I AM GRATEFUL FOR...

1. Playing with my friends.
2. A nice lunch.
3. having a nice teacher.

TODAY'S PEAKS:

Getting a late birthday present from Layla.

HOW HAPPY I FEEL: 😊 (circled)

SOMETHING AWESOME THAT HAPPENED TODAY:
DRAW OR WRITE ABOUT IT!

Lucas

21 / 1 / 2020

MON **TUE** WED THU FRI SAT SUN

TODAY I AM GRATEFUL FOR...

1. having a roof over my head.
2. having poppadoms.
3. Playing goat simulater with Ryan.

TODAY'S PEAKS:

Getting a good mark on my project.

HOW HAPPY I FEEL: 😊 😍 **😳** 😐 ☹️

SOMETHING AWESOME THAT HAPPENED TODAY:
DRAW OR WRITE ABOUT IT!

___/___/___

MON	TUE	WED	THU	FRI	SAT	SUN
○	○	○	○	○	○	○

TODAY I AM GRATEFUL FOR...

1. ....

2. ....

3. ....

TODAY'S PEAKS:
....
....

HOW HAPPY I FEEL: 😊   🥰   😳   😐   😟

SOMETHING AWESOME THAT HAPPENED TODAY:
DRAW OR WRITE ABOUT IT!

____ / ____ / ____

MON	TUE	WED	THU	FRI	SAT	SUN
○	○	○	○	○	○	○

―――――― TODAY I AM GRATEFUL FOR... ――――――

1. ....
2. ....
3. ....

TODAY'S PEAKS:
....
....

HOW HAPPY I FEEL: 😊   😍   😳   😐   ☹️

SOMETHING AWESOME THAT HAPPENED TODAY:
DRAW OR WRITE ABOUT IT!

___/ ___/ ___

| MON | TUE | WED | THU | FRI | SAT | SUN |
| O | O | O | O | O | O | O |

— TODAY I AM GRATEFUL FOR… —

1. ....
2. ....
3. ....

TODAY'S PEAKS:
....

....

HOW HAPPY I FEEL: 😊   🥰   😵   😐   😟

SOMETHING AWESOME THAT HAPPENED TODAY:
DRAW OR WRITE ABOUT IT!

____/ ____/ ____

MON	TUE	WED	THU	FRI	SAT	SUN
○	○	○	○	○	○	○

TODAY I AM GRATEFUL FOR...

1. ....
2. ....
3. ....

TODAY'S PEAKS:
....
....

HOW HAPPY I FEEL: 😊 😍 😳 😐 😟

SOMETHING AWESOME THAT HAPPENED TODAY:
DRAW OR WRITE ABOUT IT!

___ / ___ / ___

MON	TUE	WED	THU	FRI	SAT	SUN
○	○	○	○	○	○	○

TODAY I AM GRATEFUL FOR...

1. ....
2. ....
3. ....

TODAY'S PEAKS:
....
....

HOW HAPPY I FEEL: 😊   🥰   😳   😐   ☹️

SOMETHING AWESOME THAT HAPPENED TODAY:
DRAW OR WRITE ABOUT IT!

____/ ____/ ____

MON	TUE	WED	THU	FRI	SAT	SUN
○	○	○	○	○	○	○

TODAY I AM GRATEFUL FOR...

1. ....
2. ....
3. ....

TODAY'S PEAKS:
....
....

HOW HAPPY I FEEL: 😊   😍   😳   😐   😟

**SOMETHING AWESOME THAT HAPPENED TODAY:
DRAW OR WRITE ABOUT IT!**

____/ ____/ ____

MON	TUE	WED	THU	FRI	SAT	SUN
○	○	○	○	○	○	○

TODAY I AM GRATEFUL FOR...

1. ....
2. ....
3. ....

TODAY'S PEAKS:
....
....

HOW HAPPY I FEEL: 😊 😍 😵 😐 ☹️

SOMETHING AWESOME THAT HAPPENED TODAY:
DRAW OR WRITE ABOUT IT!

____ / ____ / ____

MON	TUE	WED	THU	FRI	SAT	SUN
○	○	○	○	○	○	○

TODAY I AM GRATEFUL FOR...

1. ....
2. ....
3. ....

TODAY'S PEAKS:
....
....

HOW HAPPY I FEEL: 😊 😍 🙄 😐 😟

**SOMETHING AWESOME THAT HAPPENED TODAY:
DRAW OR WRITE ABOUT IT!**

____/ ____/ ____

MON	TUE	WED	THU	FRI	SAT	SUN
○	○	○	○	○	○	○

TODAY I AM GRATEFUL FOR...

1. ....
2. ....
3. ....

TODAY'S PEAKS:
....
....

HOW HAPPY I FEEL: 😊 😍 😳 😐 😟

SOMETHING AWESOME THAT HAPPENED TODAY:
DRAW OR WRITE ABOUT IT!

____/ ____/ ____

MON	TUE	WED	THU	FRI	SAT	SUN
○	○	○	○	○	○	○

TODAY I AM GRATEFUL FOR...

1. ....
2. ....
3. ....

TODAY'S PEAKS:
....
....

HOW HAPPY I FEEL: 😊 😍 😳 😐 😟

**SOMETHING AWESOME THAT HAPPENED TODAY:
DRAW OR WRITE ABOUT IT!**

___/ ___/ ___

MON	TUE	WED	THU	FRI	SAT	SUN
○	○	○	○	○	○	○

TODAY I AM GRATEFUL FOR...

1. ....
2. ....
3. ....

TODAY'S PEAKS:
....
....

HOW HAPPY I FEEL: 😊 😍 😵 😐 ☹️

SOMETHING AWESOME THAT HAPPENED TODAY:
DRAW OR WRITE ABOUT IT!

____/ ____/ ____

MON TUE WED THU FRI SAT SUN
 ○   ○   ○   ○   ○   ○   ○

TODAY I AM GRATEFUL FOR...

1. ....
2. ....
3. ....

TODAY'S PEAKS:
....
....

HOW HAPPY I FEEL: 😊 😍 🙄 😐 😟

SOMETHING AWESOME THAT HAPPENED TODAY:
DRAW OR WRITE ABOUT IT!

____/ ____/ ____

MON	TUE	WED	THU	FRI	SAT	SUN
○	○	○	○	○	○	○

TODAY I AM GRATEFUL FOR...

1. ....
2. ....
3. ....

TODAY'S PEAKS:
....
....

HOW HAPPY I FEEL: 😊   😍   😳   😐   😟

SOMETHING AWESOME THAT HAPPENED TODAY:
DRAW OR WRITE ABOUT IT!

___/ ___/ ___

MON	TUE	WED	THU	FRI	SAT	SUN
○	○	○	○	○	○	○

TODAY I AM GRATEFUL FOR...

1. ....
2. ....
3. ....

TODAY'S PEAKS:
....
....

HOW HAPPY I FEEL: 😊 😍 😳 😐 😟

SOMETHING AWESOME THAT HAPPENED TODAY:
DRAW OR WRITE ABOUT IT!

___ / ___ / ___

MON	TUE	WED	THU	FRI	SAT	SUN
○	○	○	○	○	○	○

TODAY I AM GRATEFUL FOR...

1. ....
2. ....
3. ....

TODAY'S PEAKS:
....
....

HOW HAPPY I FEEL: 😊 😍 😵 😐 ☹️

SOMETHING AWESOME THAT HAPPENED TODAY:
DRAW OR WRITE ABOUT IT!

____/ ____/ ____

MON	TUE	WED	THU	FRI	SAT	SUN
○	○	○	○	○	○	○

TODAY I AM GRATEFUL FOR...

1. ....
2. ....
3. ....

TODAY'S PEAKS:
....
....

HOW HAPPY I FEEL: 😊 😍 😵 😐 ☹️

SOMETHING AWESOME THAT HAPPENED TODAY:
DRAW OR WRITE ABOUT IT!

____/ ____/ ____

MON	TUE	WED	THU	FRI	SAT	SUN
○	○	○	○	○	○	○

TODAY I AM GRATEFUL FOR...

1. ....
2. ....
3. ....

TODAY'S PEAKS:
....
....

HOW HAPPY I FEEL: 😊   🥰   😳   😐   😟

SOMETHING AWESOME THAT HAPPENED TODAY:
DRAW OR WRITE ABOUT IT!

___ / ___ / ___

MON	TUE	WED	THU	FRI	SAT	SUN
○	○	○	○	○	○	○

TODAY I AM GRATEFUL FOR...

1. ....
2. ....
3. ....

TODAY'S PEAKS:
....
....

HOW HAPPY I FEEL: 😊   😍   😵   😐   😟

SOMETHING AWESOME THAT HAPPENED TODAY:
DRAW OR WRITE ABOUT IT!

___/ ___/ ___

MON	TUE	WED	THU	FRI	SAT	SUN
○	○	○	○	○	○	○

— TODAY I AM GRATEFUL FOR… —

1. ....
2. ....
3. ....

TODAY'S PEAKS:
....
....

HOW HAPPY I FEEL: 😊 😍 😵 😐 ☹️

**SOMETHING AWESOME THAT HAPPENED TODAY:
DRAW OR WRITE ABOUT IT!**

___/ ___/ ___

| MON | TUE | WED | THU | FRI | SAT | SUN |
| ○ | ○ | ○ | ○ | ○ | ○ | ○ |

TODAY I AM GRATEFUL FOR...

1. ....
2. ....
3. ....

TODAY'S PEAKS:
....
....

HOW HAPPY I FEEL: 😊 😍 😵 😐 😟

**SOMETHING AWESOME THAT HAPPENED TODAY:
DRAW OR WRITE ABOUT IT!**

____/ ____/ ____

MON	TUE	WED	THU	FRI	SAT	SUN
○	○	○	○	○	○	○

TODAY I AM GRATEFUL FOR...

1. ....
2. ....
3. ....

TODAY'S PEAKS:
....
....

HOW HAPPY I FEEL: 😊 😍 😵 😐 😟

SOMETHING AWESOME THAT HAPPENED TODAY:
DRAW OR WRITE ABOUT IT!

____/ ____/ ____

MON	TUE	WED	THU	FRI	SAT	SUN
○	○	○	○	○	○	○

TODAY I AM GRATEFUL FOR...

1. ....
2. ....
3. ....

TODAY'S PEAKS:
....
....

HOW HAPPY I FEEL: 😊 😍 😵 😐 😟

**SOMETHING AWESOME THAT HAPPENED TODAY:
DRAW OR WRITE ABOUT IT!**

___/ ___/ ___

MON	TUE	WED	THU	FRI	SAT	SUN
○	○	○	○	○	○	○

TODAY I AM GRATEFUL FOR...

1. ....
2. ....
3. ....

TODAY'S PEAKS:
....
....

HOW HAPPY I FEEL: 😊   😍   😵   😐   😧

**SOMETHING AWESOME THAT HAPPENED TODAY:
DRAW OR WRITE ABOUT IT!**

____/ ____/ ____

| MON | TUE | WED | THU | FRI | SAT | SUN |
| ○ | ○ | ○ | ○ | ○ | ○ | ○ |

TODAY I AM GRATEFUL FOR...

1. ....
2. ....
3. ....

TODAY'S PEAKS:
....
....

HOW HAPPY I FEEL: 😊 😍 😳 😐 😟

SOMETHING AWESOME THAT HAPPENED TODAY:
DRAW OR WRITE ABOUT IT!

_____ / _____ / _____

MON	TUE	WED	THU	FRI	SAT	SUN
○	○	○	○	○	○	○

TODAY I AM GRATEFUL FOR...

1. ....
2. ....
3. ....

TODAY'S PEAKS:
....
....

HOW HAPPY I FEEL: 😊 😍 😵 😐 😟

**SOMETHING AWESOME THAT HAPPENED TODAY:
DRAW OR WRITE ABOUT IT!**

____/ ____/ ____

MON	TUE	WED	THU	FRI	SAT	SUN
○	○	○	○	○	○	○

──── TODAY I AM GRATEFUL FOR… ────

1. ....
2. ....
3. ....

TODAY'S PEAKS:
....
....

HOW HAPPY I FEEL: 😊   😍   😵   😐   ☹️

SOMETHING AWESOME THAT HAPPENED TODAY:
DRAW OR WRITE ABOUT IT!

____/ ____/ ____

MON	TUE	WED	THU	FRI	SAT	SUN
○	○	○	○	○	○	○

TODAY I AM GRATEFUL FOR...

1. _____

2. _____

3. _____

TODAY'S PEAKS:
_____
_____

HOW HAPPY I FEEL: 😊   😍   😵   😐   😟

SOMETHING AWESOME THAT HAPPENED TODAY:
DRAW OR WRITE ABOUT IT!

____/ ____/ ____

MON	TUE	WED	THU	FRI	SAT	SUN
○	○	○	○	○	○	○

TODAY I AM GRATEFUL FOR...

1. ....
2. ....
3. ....

TODAY'S PEAKS:
....
....

HOW HAPPY I FEEL: 😊   😍   😳   😐   😟

SOMETHING AWESOME THAT HAPPENED TODAY:
DRAW OR WRITE ABOUT IT!

____/ ____/ ____

MON	TUE	WED	THU	FRI	SAT	SUN
○	○	○	○	○	○	○

TODAY I AM GRATEFUL FOR...

1. ....

2. ....

3. ....

TODAY'S PEAKS:
....
....

HOW HAPPY I FEEL: 😊   😍   😳   😐   😟

SOMETHING AWESOME THAT HAPPENED TODAY:
DRAW OR WRITE ABOUT IT!

____/ ____/ ____

MON	TUE	WED	THU	FRI	SAT	SUN
○	○	○	○	○	○	○

TODAY I AM GRATEFUL FOR...

1. ....
2. ....
3. ....

TODAY'S PEAKS:
....
....

HOW HAPPY I FEEL: 😊   😍   😵   😐   😟

SOMETHING AWESOME THAT HAPPENED TODAY:
DRAW OR WRITE ABOUT IT!

___/ ___/ ___

| MON | TUE | WED | THU | FRI | SAT | SUN |
| ○ | ○ | ○ | ○ | ○ | ○ | ○ |

TODAY I AM GRATEFUL FOR...

1. ....

2. ....

3. ....

TODAY'S PEAKS:
....

....

HOW HAPPY I FEEL: 😊 😍 😵 😐 ☹️

SOMETHING AWESOME THAT HAPPENED TODAY:
DRAW OR WRITE ABOUT IT!

___/ ___/ ___

MON	TUE	WED	THU	FRI	SAT	SUN
○	○	○	○	○	○	○

TODAY I AM GRATEFUL FOR...

1. ....
2. ....
3. ....

TODAY'S PEAKS:
....

....

HOW HAPPY I FEEL: 😊   😍   😳   😐   😟

SOMETHING AWESOME THAT HAPPENED TODAY: DRAW OR WRITE ABOUT IT!

___/___/___

MON	TUE	WED	THU	FRI	SAT	SUN
○	○	○	○	○	○	○

TODAY I AM GRATEFUL FOR...

1. ....
2. ....
3. ....

TODAY'S PEAKS:
....
....

HOW HAPPY I FEEL: 😊 😍 😵 😐 😟

SOMETHING AWESOME THAT HAPPENED TODAY:
DRAW OR WRITE ABOUT IT!

____/ ____/ ____

MON	TUE	WED	THU	FRI	SAT	SUN
○	○	○	○	○	○	○

TODAY I AM GRATEFUL FOR...

1. ....
2. ....
3. ....

TODAY'S PEAKS:
....
....

HOW HAPPY I FEEL: 😊   😍   😳   😐   ☹️

SOMETHING AWESOME THAT HAPPENED TODAY:
DRAW OR WRITE ABOUT IT!

___/ ___/ ___

| MON | TUE | WED | THU | FRI | SAT | SUN |
| ○ | ○ | ○ | ○ | ○ | ○ | ○ |

TODAY I AM GRATEFUL FOR...

1. ....
2. ....
3. ....

TODAY'S PEAKS:
....
....

HOW HAPPY I FEEL: 😊 😍 😵 😐 😞

SOMETHING AWESOME THAT HAPPENED TODAY:
DRAW OR WRITE ABOUT IT!

____/ ____/ ____

| MON | TUE | WED | THU | FRI | SAT | SUN |
| ○ | ○ | ○ | ○ | ○ | ○ | ○ |

TODAY I AM GRATEFUL FOR...

1. ....
2. ....
3. ....

TODAY'S PEAKS:
....
....

HOW HAPPY I FEEL: 😊 😍 😳 😐 😞

SOMETHING AWESOME THAT HAPPENED TODAY:
DRAW OR WRITE ABOUT IT!

___/___/___

MON	TUE	WED	THU	FRI	SAT	SUN
○	○	○	○	○	○	○

TODAY I AM GRATEFUL FOR...

1. ....
2. ....
3. ....

TODAY'S PEAKS:
....
....

HOW HAPPY I FEEL: 😊 😍 😳 😐 😟

SOMETHING AWESOME THAT HAPPENED TODAY:
DRAW OR WRITE ABOUT IT!

___/ ___/ ___

MON	TUE	WED	THU	FRI	SAT	SUN
○	○	○	○	○	○	○

TODAY I AM GRATEFUL FOR...

1. ....
2. ....
3. ....

TODAY'S PEAKS:
....
....

HOW HAPPY I FEEL: 😊   😍   😳   😐   😟

SOMETHING AWESOME THAT HAPPENED TODAY:
DRAW OR WRITE ABOUT IT!

____/ ____/ ____

MON	TUE	WED	THU	FRI	SAT	SUN
○	○	○	○	○	○	○

TODAY I AM GRATEFUL FOR...

1. ....

2. ....

3. ....

TODAY'S PEAKS:
....
....

HOW HAPPY I FEEL: 😊   😍   😵   😐   😟

**SOMETHING AWESOME THAT HAPPENED TODAY:
DRAW OR WRITE ABOUT IT!**

____/ ____/ ____

MON	TUE	WED	THU	FRI	SAT	SUN
○	○	○	○	○	○	○

TODAY I AM GRATEFUL FOR...

1. ....
2. ....
3. ....

TODAY'S PEAKS:
....
....

HOW HAPPY I FEEL: 😊 😍 😵 😐 ☹️

SOMETHING AWESOME THAT HAPPENED TODAY:
DRAW OR WRITE ABOUT IT!

___/___/___

MON	TUE	WED	THU	FRI	SAT	SUN
○	○	○	○	○	○	○

TODAY I AM GRATEFUL FOR...

1.

2.

3.

TODAY'S PEAKS:

HOW HAPPY I FEEL: 😊 😍 😵 😐 😟

SOMETHING AWESOME THAT HAPPENED TODAY:
DRAW OR WRITE ABOUT IT!

____/ ____/ ____

MON	TUE	WED	THU	FRI	SAT	SUN
○	○	○	○	○	○	○

TODAY I AM GRATEFUL FOR...

1. ....
2. ....
3. ....

TODAY'S PEAKS:
....
....

HOW HAPPY I FEEL: 😊 😍 😵 😐 😞

SOMETHING AWESOME THAT HAPPENED TODAY:
DRAW OR WRITE ABOUT IT!

___/ ___/ ___

MON	TUE	WED	THU	FRI	SAT	SUN
○	○	○	○	○	○	○

TODAY I AM GRATEFUL FOR...

1. ....
2. ....
3. ....

TODAY'S PEAKS:
....
....

HOW HAPPY I FEEL: 😊   😍   😵   😐   ☹️

SOMETHING AWESOME THAT HAPPENED TODAY:
DRAW OR WRITE ABOUT IT!

___/ ___/ ___

MON	TUE	WED	THU	FRI	SAT	SUN
○	○	○	○	○	○	○

TODAY I AM GRATEFUL FOR...

1. ....
2. ....
3. ....

TODAY'S PEAKS:
....
....

HOW HAPPY I FEEL: 😊 😍 😵 😐 😟

SOMETHING AWESOME THAT HAPPENED TODAY:
DRAW OR WRITE ABOUT IT!

___/ ___/ ___

MON	TUE	WED	THU	FRI	SAT	SUN
○	○	○	○	○	○	○

TODAY I AM GRATEFUL FOR...

1.
2.
3.

TODAY'S PEAKS:

HOW HAPPY I FEEL: 😊 😍 😵 😐 😟

SOMETHING AWESOME THAT HAPPENED TODAY:
DRAW OR WRITE ABOUT IT!

___/ ___/ ___

MON	TUE	WED	THU	FRI	SAT	SUN
○	○	○	○	○	○	○

TODAY I AM GRATEFUL FOR...

1. ....
2. ....
3. ....

TODAY'S PEAKS:
....
....

HOW HAPPY I FEEL: 😊 😍 🙄 😐 😟

**SOMETHING AWESOME THAT HAPPENED TODAY:
DRAW OR WRITE ABOUT IT!**

___/ ___/ ___

MON	TUE	WED	THU	FRI	SAT	SUN
○	○	○	○	○	○	○

— TODAY I AM GRATEFUL FOR... —

1. ....
2. ....
3. ....

TODAY'S PEAKS:
....
....

HOW HAPPY I FEEL: 😊   😍   😵   😐   😟

SOMETHING AWESOME THAT HAPPENED TODAY:
DRAW OR WRITE ABOUT IT!

____/ ____/ ____

MON	TUE	WED	THU	FRI	SAT	SUN
○	○	○	○	○	○	○

TODAY I AM GRATEFUL FOR...

1. ....
2. ....
3. ....

TODAY'S PEAKS:
....
....

HOW HAPPY I FEEL: 😊   😍   😵   😐   ☹️

SOMETHING AWESOME THAT HAPPENED TODAY:
DRAW OR WRITE ABOUT IT!

___ / ___ / ___

MON	TUE	WED	THU	FRI	SAT	SUN
○	○	○	○	○	○	○

TODAY I AM GRATEFUL FOR...

1. ....
2. ....
3. ....

TODAY'S PEAKS:
....
....

HOW HAPPY I FEEL: 😊   😍   😵   😐   😟

**SOMETHING AWESOME THAT HAPPENED TODAY:
DRAW OR WRITE ABOUT IT!**

____/ ____/ ____

MON	TUE	WED	THU	FRI	SAT	SUN
○	○	○	○	○	○	○

TODAY I AM GRATEFUL FOR...

1. ....
2. ....
3. ....

TODAY'S PEAKS:
....
....

HOW HAPPY I FEEL: 😊   😍   😵   😐   😟

SOMETHING AWESOME THAT HAPPENED TODAY:
DRAW OR WRITE ABOUT IT!

___ / ___ / ___

MON TUE WED THU FRI SAT SUN
 ○   ○   ○   ○   ○   ○   ○

TODAY I AM GRATEFUL FOR...

1. ....
2. ....
3. ....

TODAY'S PEAKS:
....
....

HOW HAPPY I FEEL: 😊 😍 😵 😐 😟

SOMETHING AWESOME THAT HAPPENED TODAY:
DRAW OR WRITE ABOUT IT!

____/ ____/ ____

MON	TUE	WED	THU	FRI	SAT	SUN
○	○	○	○	○	○	○

--- TODAY I AM GRATEFUL FOR... ---

1. ....
2. ....
3. ....

TODAY'S PEAKS:
....
....

HOW HAPPY I FEEL: 😊   🥰   😵   😐   ☹️

SOMETHING AWESOME THAT HAPPENED TODAY:
DRAW OR WRITE ABOUT IT!

____/ ____/ ____

MON	TUE	WED	THU	FRI	SAT	SUN
○	○	○	○	○	○	○

TODAY I AM GRATEFUL FOR...

1. ....
2. ....
3. ....

TODAY'S PEAKS:
....
....

HOW HAPPY I FEEL: 😊   😍   😵   😐   😞

SOMETHING AWESOME THAT HAPPENED TODAY:
DRAW OR WRITE ABOUT IT!

____/ ____/ ____

MON	TUE	WED	THU	FRI	SAT	SUN
○	○	○	○	○	○	○

TODAY I AM GRATEFUL FOR...

1. ....
2. ....
3. ....

TODAY'S PEAKS:
....
....

HOW HAPPY I FEEL: 😊 😍 😵 😐 ☹️

**SOMETHING AWESOME THAT HAPPENED TODAY:
DRAW OR WRITE ABOUT IT!**

____/ ____/ ____

MON	TUE	WED	THU	FRI	SAT	SUN
○	○	○	○	○	○	○

TODAY I AM GRATEFUL FOR...

1.
2.
3.

TODAY'S PEAKS:

HOW HAPPY I FEEL: 😊 😍 😳 😐 ☹️

SOMETHING AWESOME THAT HAPPENED TODAY:
DRAW OR WRITE ABOUT IT!

____/ ____/ ____

MON	TUE	WED	THU	FRI	SAT	SUN
○	○	○	○	○	○	○

TODAY I AM GRATEFUL FOR...

1. ....
2. ....
3. ....

TODAY'S PEAKS:
....
....

HOW HAPPY I FEEL: 😊   😍   😳   😐   ☹️

**SOMETHING AWESOME THAT HAPPENED TODAY:
DRAW OR WRITE ABOUT IT!**

____/ ____/ ____

MON	TUE	WED	THU	FRI	SAT	SUN
○	○	○	○	○	○	○

TODAY I AM GRATEFUL FOR...

1. ....
2. ....
3. ....

TODAY'S PEAKS:
....
....

HOW HAPPY I FEEL: 😊 🥰 😵 😐 😟

SOMETHING AWESOME THAT HAPPENED TODAY:
DRAW OR WRITE ABOUT IT!

____/ ____/ ____

MON	TUE	WED	THU	FRI	SAT	SUN
○	○	○	○	○	○	○

TODAY I AM GRATEFUL FOR...

1. ....
2. ....
3. ....

TODAY'S PEAKS:
....
....

HOW HAPPY I FEEL: 😊 😍 😵 😐 😟

**SOMETHING AWESOME THAT HAPPENED TODAY:
DRAW OR WRITE ABOUT IT!**

____/ ____/ ____

MON	TUE	WED	THU	FRI	SAT	SUN
○	○	○	○	○	○	○

--- TODAY I AM GRATEFUL FOR... ---

1. ....
2. ....
3. ....

TODAY'S PEAKS:
....
....

HOW HAPPY I FEEL: 😊   😍   😵   😐   😟

SOMETHING AWESOME THAT HAPPENED TODAY:
DRAW OR WRITE ABOUT IT!

___ / ___ / ___

MON	TUE	WED	THU	FRI	SAT	SUN
○	○	○	○	○	○	○

TODAY I AM GRATEFUL FOR...

1. ....
2. ....
3. ....

TODAY'S PEAKS:
....
....

HOW HAPPY I FEEL: 😊 😍 😵 😐 ☹️

SOMETHING AWESOME THAT HAPPENED TODAY:
DRAW OR WRITE ABOUT IT!

_____/ _____/ _____

MON	TUE	WED	THU	FRI	SAT	SUN
○	○	○	○	○	○	○

TODAY I AM GRATEFUL FOR...

1. ....
2. ....
3. ....

TODAY'S PEAKS:
....
....

HOW HAPPY I FEEL: 😊   😍   😵   😐   ☹️

SOMETHING AWESOME THAT HAPPENED TODAY:
DRAW OR WRITE ABOUT IT!

___/___/___

MON	TUE	WED	THU	FRI	SAT	SUN
○	○	○	○	○	○	○

TODAY I AM GRATEFUL FOR...

1. ....
2. ....
3. ....

TODAY'S PEAKS:
....
....

HOW HAPPY I FEEL: 😊 😍 😵 😐 😟

SOMETHING AWESOME THAT HAPPENED TODAY:
DRAW OR WRITE ABOUT IT!

____/ ____/ ____

MON   TUE   WED   THU   FRI   SAT   SUN
 ○   ○   ○   ○   ○   ○   ○

——————— TODAY I AM GRATEFUL FOR... ———————

1. ....

2. ....

3. ....

TODAY'S PEAKS:
....
....

HOW HAPPY I FEEL: 😊   😍   😵   😐   😟

SOMETHING AWESOME THAT HAPPENED TODAY:
DRAW OR WRITE ABOUT IT!

____/ ____/ ____

MON	TUE	WED	THU	FRI	SAT	SUN
○	○	○	○	○	○	○

TODAY I AM GRATEFUL FOR...

1. ....
2. ....
3. ....

TODAY'S PEAKS:
....
....

HOW HAPPY I FEEL: 😊 😍 😳 😐 😟

**SOMETHING AWESOME THAT HAPPENED TODAY:
DRAW OR WRITE ABOUT IT!**

___ / ___ / ___

MON	TUE	WED	THU	FRI	SAT	SUN
○	○	○	○	○	○	○

TODAY I AM GRATEFUL FOR...

1. ....
2. ....
3. ....

TODAY'S PEAKS:
....
....

HOW HAPPY I FEEL: 😊 😍 😵 😐 ☹️

**SOMETHING AWESOME THAT HAPPENED TODAY:
DRAW OR WRITE ABOUT IT!**

____/ ____/ ____

MON	TUE	WED	THU	FRI	SAT	SUN
○	○	○	○	○	○	○

TODAY I AM GRATEFUL FOR...

1.
2.
3.

TODAY'S PEAKS:

HOW HAPPY I FEEL: 😊 😍 😵 😐 😟

SOMETHING AWESOME THAT HAPPENED TODAY:
DRAW OR WRITE ABOUT IT!

___/ ___/ ___

MON	TUE	WED	THU	FRI	SAT	SUN
○	○	○	○	○	○	○

TODAY I AM GRATEFUL FOR...

1. ....
2. ....
3. ....

TODAY'S PEAKS:
....
....

HOW HAPPY I FEEL: 😊 😍 😵 😐 😟

**SOMETHING AWESOME THAT HAPPENED TODAY:
DRAW OR WRITE ABOUT IT!**

___/___/___

MON	TUE	WED	THU	FRI	SAT	SUN
○	○	○	○	○	○	○

TODAY I AM GRATEFUL FOR...

1. ....
2. ....
3. ....

TODAY'S PEAKS:
....
....

HOW HAPPY I FEEL: 😊   😍   🙄   😐   😟

SOMETHING AWESOME THAT HAPPENED TODAY:
DRAW OR WRITE ABOUT IT!

____/ ____/ ____

| MON | TUE | WED | THU | FRI | SAT | SUN |
| O | O | O | O | O | O | O |

—————— TODAY I AM GRATEFUL FOR... ——————

1. ....
2. ....
3. ....

TODAY'S PEAKS:
....
....

HOW HAPPY I FEEL: 😊   😍   😵   😐   ☹️

SOMETHING AWESOME THAT HAPPENED TODAY:
DRAW OR WRITE ABOUT IT!

____/ ____/ ____

MON	TUE	WED	THU	FRI	SAT	SUN
○	○	○	○	○	○	○

TODAY I AM GRATEFUL FOR...

1. ....
2. ....
3. ....

TODAY'S PEAKS:
....
....

HOW HAPPY I FEEL: 😊 😍 😵 😐 ☹️

SOMETHING AWESOME THAT HAPPENED TODAY:
DRAW OR WRITE ABOUT IT!

____ / ____ / ____

MON   TUE   WED   THU   FRI   SAT   SUN
 ○   ○   ○   ○   ○   ○   ○

TODAY I AM GRATEFUL FOR...

1. ....
2. ....
3. ....

TODAY'S PEAKS:
....
....

HOW HAPPY I FEEL:

**SOMETHING AWESOME THAT HAPPENED TODAY:
DRAW OR WRITE ABOUT IT!**

____/ ____/ ____

MON	TUE	WED	THU	FRI	SAT	SUN
○	○	○	○	○	○	○

——— TODAY I AM GRATEFUL FOR… ———

1. ....
2. ....
3. ....

TODAY'S PEAKS:
....
....

HOW HAPPY I FEEL: 😊 😍 😵 😐 😟

**SOMETHING AWESOME THAT HAPPENED TODAY:
DRAW OR WRITE ABOUT IT!**

____/ ____/ ____

MON	TUE	WED	THU	FRI	SAT	SUN
○	○	○	○	○	○	○

TODAY I AM GRATEFUL FOR...

1. ....
2. ....
3. ....

TODAY'S PEAKS:
....
....

HOW HAPPY I FEEL: 😊 😍 😵 😐 😟

SOMETHING AWESOME THAT HAPPENED TODAY:
DRAW OR WRITE ABOUT IT!

____/ ____/ ____

MON	TUE	WED	THU	FRI	SAT	SUN
○	○	○	○	○	○	○

TODAY I AM GRATEFUL FOR...

1. ....
2. ....
3. ....

TODAY'S PEAKS:
....
....

HOW HAPPY I FEEL: 😊 😍 😳 😐 ☹️

SOMETHING AWESOME THAT HAPPENED TODAY:
DRAW OR WRITE ABOUT IT!

___/___/___

MON	TUE	WED	THU	FRI	SAT	SUN
○	○	○	○	○	○	○

TODAY I AM GRATEFUL FOR...

1. ....
2. ....
3. ....

TODAY'S PEAKS:
....
....

HOW HAPPY I FEEL: 😊 😍 😳 😐 😟

**SOMETHING AWESOME THAT HAPPENED TODAY:
DRAW OR WRITE ABOUT IT!**

___ / ___ / ___

MON	TUE	WED	THU	FRI	SAT	SUN
○	○	○	○	○	○	○

TODAY I AM GRATEFUL FOR...

1. ....
2. ....
3. ....

TODAY'S PEAKS:
....
....

HOW HAPPY I FEEL: 😊 😍 😵 😐 ☹️

SOMETHING AWESOME THAT HAPPENED TODAY:
DRAW OR WRITE ABOUT IT!

____/ ____/ ____

MON	TUE	WED	THU	FRI	SAT	SUN
○	○	○	○	○	○	○

TODAY I AM GRATEFUL FOR...

1. ....
2. ....
3. ....

TODAY'S PEAKS:
....
....

HOW HAPPY I FEEL: 😊 😍 😵 😐 😟

SOMETHING AWESOME THAT HAPPENED TODAY:
DRAW OR WRITE ABOUT IT!

____ / ____ / ____

MON	TUE	WED	THU	FRI	SAT	SUN
○	○	○	○	○	○	○

TODAY I AM GRATEFUL FOR...

1. ....
2. ....
3. ....

TODAY'S PEAKS:
....
....

HOW HAPPY I FEEL: 😊 😍 😵 😐 ☹️

**SOMETHING AWESOME THAT HAPPENED TODAY:
DRAW OR WRITE ABOUT IT!**

____/ ____/ ____

MON	TUE	WED	THU	FRI	SAT	SUN
○	○	○	○	○	○	○

TODAY I AM GRATEFUL FOR...

1. ....
2. ....
3. ....

TODAY'S PEAKS:
....
....

HOW HAPPY I FEEL: 😊   😍   😳   😐   😟

SOMETHING AWESOME THAT HAPPENED TODAY:
DRAW OR WRITE ABOUT IT!

____/ ____/ ____

MON	TUE	WED	THU	FRI	SAT	SUN
○	○	○	○	○	○	○

TODAY I AM GRATEFUL FOR...

1. ....
2. ....
3. ....

TODAY'S PEAKS:
....
....

HOW HAPPY I FEEL: 😊   😍   😳   😐   ☹️

SOMETHING AWESOME THAT HAPPENED TODAY:
DRAW OR WRITE ABOUT IT!

___/___/___

MON	TUE	WED	THU	FRI	SAT	SUN
○	○	○	○	○	○	○

TODAY I AM GRATEFUL FOR...

1. ....
2. ....
3. ....

TODAY'S PEAKS:
....
....

HOW HAPPY I FEEL: 😊 😍 😵 😐 😟

SOMETHING AWESOME THAT HAPPENED TODAY:
DRAW OR WRITE ABOUT IT!

____/ ____/ ____

MON	TUE	WED	THU	FRI	SAT	SUN
○	○	○	○	○	○	○

TODAY I AM GRATEFUL FOR...

1. ....
2. ....
3. ....

TODAY'S PEAKS:
....
....

HOW HAPPY I FEEL: 😊 😍 😵 😐 😟

**SOMETHING AWESOME THAT HAPPENED TODAY:
DRAW OR WRITE ABOUT IT!**

___/___/___

MON	TUE	WED	THU	FRI	SAT	SUN
○	○	○	○	○	○	○

TODAY I AM GRATEFUL FOR...

1. ....
2. ....
3. ....

TODAY'S PEAKS:
....
....

HOW HAPPY I FEEL: 😊 😍 😵 😐 😟

SOMETHING AWESOME THAT HAPPENED TODAY:
DRAW OR WRITE ABOUT IT!

____/ ____/ ____

MON	TUE	WED	THU	FRI	SAT	SUN
○	○	○	○	○	○	○

TODAY I AM GRATEFUL FOR...

1. ....
2. ....
3. ....

TODAY'S PEAKS:
....
....

HOW HAPPY I FEEL: 😊 😍 😵 😐 😟

**SOMETHING AWESOME THAT HAPPENED TODAY:
DRAW OR WRITE ABOUT IT!**

_____ / _____ / _____

MON	TUE	WED	THU	FRI	SAT	SUN
○	○	○	○	○	○	○

TODAY I AM GRATEFUL FOR...

1. ....
2. ....
3. ....

TODAY'S PEAKS:
....
....

HOW HAPPY I FEEL: 😊   😍   😵   😐   ☹️

SOMETHING AWESOME THAT HAPPENED TODAY:
DRAW OR WRITE ABOUT IT!

____/ ____/ ____

| MON | TUE | WED | THU | FRI | SAT | SUN |
| ○ | ○ | ○ | ○ | ○ | ○ | ○ |

TODAY I AM GRATEFUL FOR...

1. ....
2. ....
3. ....

TODAY'S PEAKS:
....
....

HOW HAPPY I FEEL: 😊   😍   😵   😐   ☹️

SOMETHING AWESOME THAT HAPPENED TODAY:
DRAW OR WRITE ABOUT IT!

___ / ___ / ___

MON	TUE	WED	THU	FRI	SAT	SUN
○	○	○	○	○	○	○

TODAY I AM GRATEFUL FOR...

1. ....
2. ....
3. ....

TODAY'S PEAKS:
....
....

HOW HAPPY I FEEL: 😊 😍 😵 😐 😟

SOMETHING AWESOME THAT HAPPENED TODAY:
DRAW OR WRITE ABOUT IT!

___/ ___/ ___

MON	TUE	WED	THU	FRI	SAT	SUN
○	○	○	○	○	○	○

TODAY I AM GRATEFUL FOR...

1. ....
2. ....
3. ....

TODAY'S PEAKS:
....
....

HOW HAPPY I FEEL: 😊 😍 😵 😐 😟

SOMETHING AWESOME THAT HAPPENED TODAY:
DRAW OR WRITE ABOUT IT!

___/___/___

| MON | TUE | WED | THU | FRI | SAT | SUN |
| ○ | ○ | ○ | ○ | ○ | ○ | ○ |

TODAY I AM GRATEFUL FOR...

1. ....
2. ....
3. ....

TODAY'S PEAKS:
....
....

HOW HAPPY I FEEL: 😋   😍   😵   😐   😟

SOMETHING AWESOME THAT HAPPENED TODAY:
DRAW OR WRITE ABOUT IT!

_____/ _____/ _____

MON	TUE	WED	THU	FRI	SAT	SUN
○	○	○	○	○	○	○

TODAY I AM GRATEFUL FOR...

1. ....
2. ....
3. ....

TODAY'S PEAKS:
....
....

HOW HAPPY I FEEL: 😊 😍 😳 😐 😟

SOMETHING AWESOME THAT HAPPENED TODAY:
DRAW OR WRITE ABOUT IT!

____/ ____/ ____

MON TUE WED THU FRI SAT SUN
 ○   ○   ○   ○   ○   ○   ○

TODAY I AM GRATEFUL FOR...

1. ....
2. ....
3. ....

TODAY'S PEAKS:
....
....

HOW HAPPY I FEEL: 😊 😍 😵 😐 ☹️

SOMETHING AWESOME THAT HAPPENED TODAY:
DRAW OR WRITE ABOUT IT!

___/___/___

MON   TUE   WED   THU   FRI   SAT   SUN
 ○   ○   ○   ○   ○   ○   ○

TODAY I AM GRATEFUL FOR...

1. ....
2. ....
3. ....

TODAY'S PEAKS:
....
....

HOW HAPPY I FEEL: 😊   😍   😳   😐   😞

SOMETHING AWESOME THAT HAPPENED TODAY:
DRAW OR WRITE ABOUT IT!

___/___/___

MON	TUE	WED	THU	FRI	SAT	SUN
○	○	○	○	○	○	○

TODAY I AM GRATEFUL FOR...

1. ....
2. ....
3. ....

TODAY'S PEAKS:
....
....

HOW HAPPY I FEEL: 😊 😍 😵 😐 😟

SOMETHING AWESOME THAT HAPPENED TODAY:
DRAW OR WRITE ABOUT IT!

___/ ___/ ___

MON	TUE	WED	THU	FRI	SAT	SUN
○	○	○	○	○	○	○

TODAY I AM GRATEFUL FOR...

1. ....
2. ....
3. ....

TODAY'S PEAKS:
....
....

HOW HAPPY I FEEL: 😊   😍   😳   😐   ☹️

SOMETHING AWESOME THAT HAPPENED TODAY:
DRAW OR WRITE ABOUT IT!

____/ ____/ ____

MON TUE WED THU FRI SAT SUN
 ○   ○   ○   ○   ○   ○   ○

──────── TODAY I AM GRATEFUL FOR... ────────

1. ....
2. ....
3. ....

TODAY'S PEAKS:
....
....

HOW HAPPY I FEEL: 😊   😍   😵   😐   😟

SOMETHING AWESOME THAT HAPPENED TODAY:
DRAW OR WRITE ABOUT IT!

___/ ___/ ___

MON	TUE	WED	THU	FRI	SAT	SUN
○	○	○	○	○	○	○

TODAY I AM GRATEFUL FOR...

1. ....
2. ....
3. ....

TODAY'S PEAKS:
....
....

HOW HAPPY I FEEL: 😊   😍   🙄   😐   😟

SOMETHING AWESOME THAT HAPPENED TODAY:
DRAW OR WRITE ABOUT IT!

____/ ____/ ____

MON	TUE	WED	THU	FRI	SAT	SUN
○	○	○	○	○	○	○

―――― TODAY I AM GRATEFUL FOR... ――――

1. ....

2. ....

3. ....

TODAY'S PEAKS:
....

....

HOW HAPPY I FEEL: 😊   🥰   😵   😐   ☹️

SOMETHING AWESOME THAT HAPPENED TODAY:
DRAW OR WRITE ABOUT IT!

___/ ___/ ___

MON	TUE	WED	THU	FRI	SAT	SUN
○	○	○	○	○	○	○

TODAY I AM GRATEFUL FOR...

1. ....
2. ....
3. ....

TODAY'S PEAKS:
....
....

HOW HAPPY I FEEL: 😊 😍 😵 😐 😟

SOMETHING AWESOME THAT HAPPENED TODAY:
DRAW OR WRITE ABOUT IT!

___/ ___/ ___

MON	TUE	WED	THU	FRI	SAT	SUN
○	○	○	○	○	○	○

—— TODAY I AM GRATEFUL FOR... ——

1. ....
2. ....
3. ....

TODAY'S PEAKS:
....
....

HOW HAPPY I FEEL: 😊 😍 😵 😐 😟

SOMETHING AWESOME THAT HAPPENED TODAY:
DRAW OR WRITE ABOUT IT!

___ / ___ / ___

MON   TUE   WED   THU   FRI   SAT   SUN
 ○   ○   ○   ○   ○   ○   ○

― TODAY I AM GRATEFUL FOR... ―

1. ....
2. ....
3. ....

TODAY'S PEAKS:
....
....

HOW HAPPY I FEEL: 😊   😍   😳   😐   ☹️

SOMETHING AWESOME THAT HAPPENED TODAY:
DRAW OR WRITE ABOUT IT!

___/___/___

MON	TUE	WED	THU	FRI	SAT	SUN
○	○	○	○	○	○	○

TODAY I AM GRATEFUL FOR...

1. ....
2. ....
3. ....

TODAY'S PEAKS:
....
....

HOW HAPPY I FEEL: 😊 😍 😵 😐 ☹️

SOMETHING AWESOME THAT HAPPENED TODAY:
DRAW OR WRITE ABOUT IT!

____/ ____/ ____

| MON | TUE | WED | THU | FRI | SAT | SUN |
| ○ | ○ | ○ | ○ | ○ | ○ | ○ |

TODAY I AM GRATEFUL FOR...

1. ....
2. ....
3. ....

TODAY'S PEAKS:
....
....

HOW HAPPY I FEEL: 😊   😍   😵   😐   ☹️

**SOMETHING AWESOME THAT HAPPENED TODAY:
DRAW OR WRITE ABOUT IT!**

____/ ____/ ____

MON TUE WED THU FRI SAT SUN
 ○   ○   ○   ○   ○   ○   ○

TODAY I AM GRATEFUL FOR...

1. ....
2. ....
3. ....

TODAY'S PEAKS:
....
....

HOW HAPPY I FEEL: 😊 😍 😵 😐 😟

SOMETHING AWESOME THAT HAPPENED TODAY:
DRAW OR WRITE ABOUT IT!

___/ ___/ ___

MON	TUE	WED	THU	FRI	SAT	SUN
○	○	○	○	○	○	○

TODAY I AM GRATEFUL FOR...

1. ....
2. ....
3. ....

TODAY'S PEAKS:
....
....

HOW HAPPY I FEEL: 😊 😍 😳 😐 ☹️

SOMETHING AWESOME THAT HAPPENED TODAY:
DRAW OR WRITE ABOUT IT!

CPSIA information can be obtained
at www.ICGtesting.com
Printed in the USA
LVHW101550060120
642663LV00018B/1229/P